Fundamental

BASEBALL

Coach Don Geng, Coach Steve Scherber, and the following athletes were photographed for this book:
A.J. Capewell,
Matt Cavanaugh,
John Dittberner,
Ben Doran,
Blake Dotson,
Christian Edwards,
Mike Griffin,
Brandon Hammergren,
Kathryn Hetherington,
Michael Honsa,
Jay Johnson,
Mike Killeen,
Dan Lewer,
Tony Liuzzi,
Melissa Peterson,
Dave Shelley,
Andy Williams,
Rob Worthington.

Fundamental
BASEBALL

Don Geng

Photographs by Andy King

Lerner Publications Company ● Minneapolis

To all my mentors who have continued to be inspirations: My coaches for whom I've played and served, my teachers, and my parents.

Library of Congress Cataloging-in-Publication Data

Geng, Don.
    Fundamental Baseball / Don Geng ;
photographs by Andy King.
        p.   cm. — (Fundamental sports)
    Includes bibliographical references (p.) and index.
    Summary: Uses photographs of young athletes to demonstrate techniques of the basic skills involved in fielding, throwing, hitting, and baserunning.
        ISBN 0-8225-3455-X
    1. Baseball—Juvenile literature. [1. Baseball.] I. King, Andy, ill. II. Title. III. Series.
GV867.5.G46 1995
796.357—dc20   95-2017

Manufactured in the United States of America

1 2 3 4 5 6 I/H 00 99 98 97 96 95

The Fundamental Sports series was conceptualized by editor Julie Jensen, designed by graphic artist Michael Tacheny, and composed on a Macintosh computer by Robert Mauzy.

Photo Acknowledgments
Photographs are reproduced with the permission of: pp. 7, 13 (top), Toronto Blue Jays; pp. 9, 10 (top), Independent Picture Service; p. 10 (bottom), Courtesy of the Boston Public Library, Print Department; pp.11 (both), 13 (bottom), National Baseball Hall of Fame and Museum, Cooperstown, N.Y.; p. 12, John Doman/St. Paul Pioneer Press; p. 25, Gregory Drezdzon/Seattle Mariners.

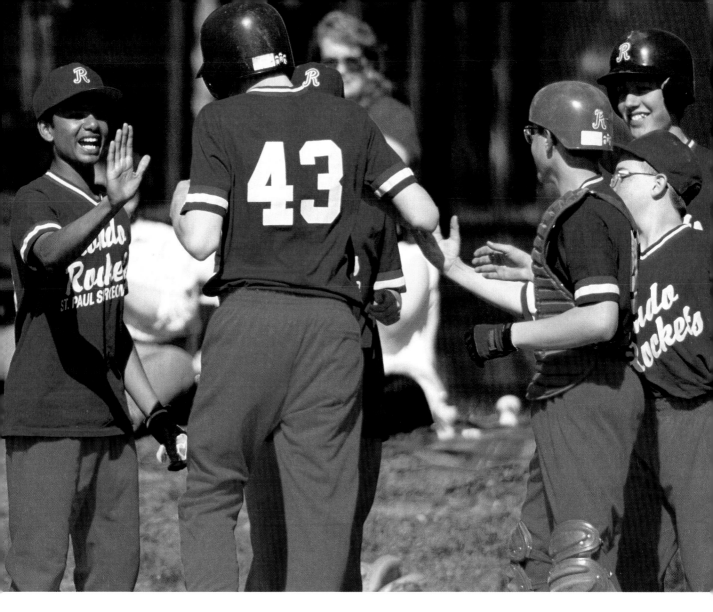

Contents

A Note From Paul Molitor

Since I began playing at the age of five, baseball has given me a great life. I have had the thrills of being on teams that were St. Paul (Minnesota) City Champs at St. Luke's Grade School, state champions at Attucks Brooks American Legion and Cretin High School, Big Ten champs at the University of Minnesota, and World Champions for the Toronto Blue Jays. But more important than all of these championships have been the great friends, experiences, and memories. Your own friendships, experiences, and even championships, will become a part of you as your love for the game grows.

But a love of the game doesn't just happen—you have to have the desire to give your best effort whenever you play baseball, whether it's in the backyard, black-topped playground, street, or manicured playing diamond. You have to believe in yourself, like the early 1900s player Wee Willie Keeler did. Only 5 feet, 4 inches tall and 140 pounds, Willie still has the fifth highest lifetime batting average in the history of major league baseball. You have to believe that nothing will stop your development—not size, not background, not coaching, not equipment.

Is believing in yourself easy? It wasn't for me. I remember crying, sulking, and going off by myself when I had a bad game or made a bad play at a crucial time. How can you avoid these negative, wasteful emotions?

Set goals, long term and short term. Commit yourself to the idea that you will work harder than anyone. You will listen better, practice the details, and *never* let yourself get discouraged. You will set short-term goals like, "I'll get a hit next time," or "I'll take 50 extra swings in my basement."

Try to learn by watching and then imitating the most successful players, whether they are your teammates, local stars, or a favorite professional player. Here's what I do. I take out a videotape of (major leaguer) Tony Gwynn and watch him hit over and over until I memorize his style. Then I practice in my mind, trying to see myself become Tony, imitating his success. Then I go into the batting cage and try to copy his quiet hands and patience at the plate. I try to wait until the last second and rocket a line drive to the opposite field the way Tony does. Try this technique—it works!

If you're lucky, you'll have as many great coaches as I did, and a parent or another family member who encourages and supports you. However, you may not be so lucky as to have everything go your way. Don't let this stop you. Great players have come from disadvantaged backgrounds. Who knows? You may be the next star!

As you improve, keep humble and keep striving to become better. Don't become cocky or too satisfied with your success. Perhaps my pet peeve is "trash talking"—the players who strut after a home run or who taunt a strike-out victim. In my opinion, this behavior has no place in baseball. Why not? Study the 160-year history of the game. No matter how good a player may become, a better player will always surface.

To escape the pressure of teammates, fans, parents, coaches, and opponents, learn to take pleasure in the game of baseball and your efforts. I have found that by preparing fully, practicing hard, dedicating myself, and striving to use the blessings of God-given talent, pressure no longer controls me. I can relax and devote all my energy and concentration to coming through in the clutch. If you dedicate yourself, you too will relax and find pleasure in being the best you can be.

Finally, play hard, but play cleanly and within the rules of the game. Play and practice wholeheartedly, with as much enthusiasm as you have.

I wish each and every one of you success in both baseball and your life. Commit yourself to a goal and strive to reach it. Have fun and take pleasure in your efforts. Take care and God bless!

Paul Molitor
1993 World Series
Most Valuable Player

How This Game Got Started

The history of baseball is a fascinating story that reflects the development of America itself. Although baseball has seen many changes throughout its history, more has remained constant than has changed.

The game has always involved two teams playing on a large field on which there are four bases. The teams take turns batting (trying to hit a ball with a bat) and playing in the field. A player on the team at bat tries to hit a ball thrown by one of the players on the fielding team. If the ball is hit, the batter tries to score a run by touching all the bases. The fielders' objective is to prevent the batter's team from scoring runs.

Baseball's origins aren't completely known. Baseball may have evolved from an English game called *rounders,* in which players hit pitched balls with

This woodcut illustration from Robin Carver's 1834 book, *Book of Sports,* shows children playing rounders.

Alexander Cartwright

bats. Rounders was popular in England during the 1600s. Like baseball, a player hit a ball with a bat and ran around four bases. Unlike baseball, the players in the field threw the ball at the runner to prevent a score. American colonists in the 1700s played rounders, but they began to call the game "base ball."

Until the mid-1800s, baseball was played by different rules in different areas. Some historians believe that players in New York City made the most significant rule change in the 1830s or 1840s when they began touching the runner with the ball in their hands (a **tag**), rather than throwing the ball at the runner. Alexander Cartwright created the first organized system of playing baseball in 1845 when he formed a club—the Knickerbocker Base Ball Club of New York—just for playing baseball. He also wrote a rule book for the sport. According to his rule book, players made a **putout** by tagging a runner and the distance between bases was set at 90 feet.

The Knickerbocker Nine were members of Alexander Cartwright's Base Ball Club of New York.

Baseball's rules evolved throughout the 1800s. For example, a rule was accepted in 1859 that ended the game after 9 **innings** if one team had more runs than the other. Before that, the first team to score 21 runs won. Players could pitch overhand after an 1884 rule change.

Baseball grew in popularity in the late 1800s, both during and after the Civil War. Soldiers from all over the United States learned the game from Northern soldiers who played baseball during breaks in the fighting. In 1869 the Cincinnati Red Stockings' owners paid all their baseball players, making them the first professionals. The National League began in 1876 with eight pro teams. Five other leagues sprang up briefly to compete with the National League but all failed until the American League was formed in 1901. Three more leagues failed after 1901.

Baseball's history includes contributions from women, Canadians, Latin Americans, and African Americans. Formal women's teams began in the 1870s at colleges such as Vassar and Smith. Starting in 1943 and throughout World War II, the All American Girls Professional Baseball League captured fan interest for 12 years.

Baseball also was a part of America's segregated past. Once, few African Americans were permitted to play with white players. Black players played in their own leagues, called the Negro Leagues. There were many great black players, such as Josh Gibson, Satchel Paige, and Rube Foster to name a few. In 1947 Jackie Robinson became the first black man to play in

Babe Ruth held the major league record for home runs in a career (714) from 1935 . . .

. . . until Hank Aaron hit his 715th home run in 1974. Aaron retired in 1976 with 755 homers.

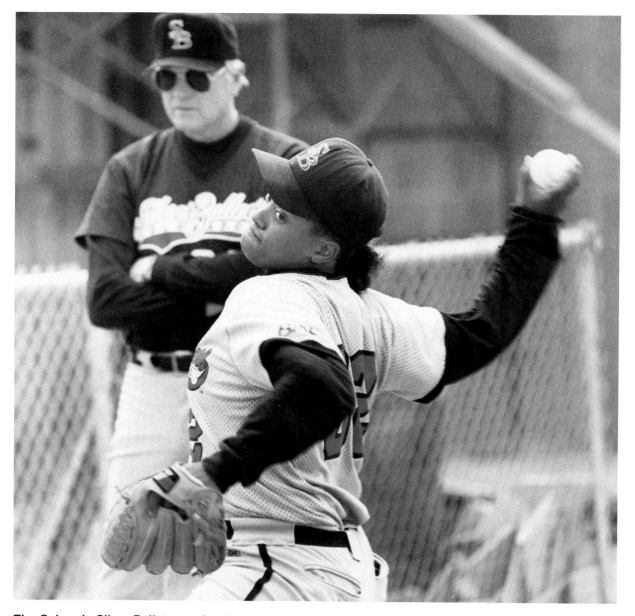

The Colorado Silver Bullets, a minor league team made up entirely of women, played other minor league teams in 1994.

major leagues. Although most of his teammates on the Brooklyn Dodgers supported him, Robinson endured many ugly taunts and threats. He overcame these obstacles, however, and was the National League Rookie of the Year in 1947, and the National League Most Valuable Player in 1949. Most important, he led the way into the major leagues for thousands of other black players.

Baseball has flourished outside of the United States also. The Dominican Republic, Canada, Japan, Mexico, Cuba, Puerto Rico, and Nicaragua have rich baseball traditions. Many outstanding players, from Hall of Famer Roberto Clemente to modern-day star Roberto Alomar, are Hispanic.

If you want to provoke an interesting conversation, ask someone what his or her favorite baseball memory is. Perhaps it was watching Don Larson's perfect game in the 1956 World Series. Or Joe Carter's dramatic home run in the 1993 Series. Maybe your friend's favorite memory is when he struck out five batters in a Little League game, or when she first completed a double play. What's your favorite baseball memory?

Roberto Alomar helped the Toronto Blue Jays win the World Series in 1992 and 1993.

Ty Cobb, a star in organized baseball's early days, developed nine different ways to slide into base.

BASICS

Equipment

To play baseball, you will need a bat, a ball, and a glove.

● *The Ball*

In baseball's earliest days, the baseballs themselves were homemade items made from twisted yarn covered by calfskin. Now, baseballs are manufactured by machines.

A baseball is 9 to 9¼ inches around and weighs 5 to 5¼ ounces. The white cowhide (or synthetic leather) cover is stitched with heavy red thread. Underneath the covering is a small cork center surrounded by two layers of rubber and three layers of yarn.

● *The Bat*

A bat is a long, smooth piece of wood —usually ash—or aluminum. The first baseball bats might have been made

Inside a Baseball

White woolen yarn   Cork

Blue-gray woolen yarn   Black rubber

Cowhide   Red rubber

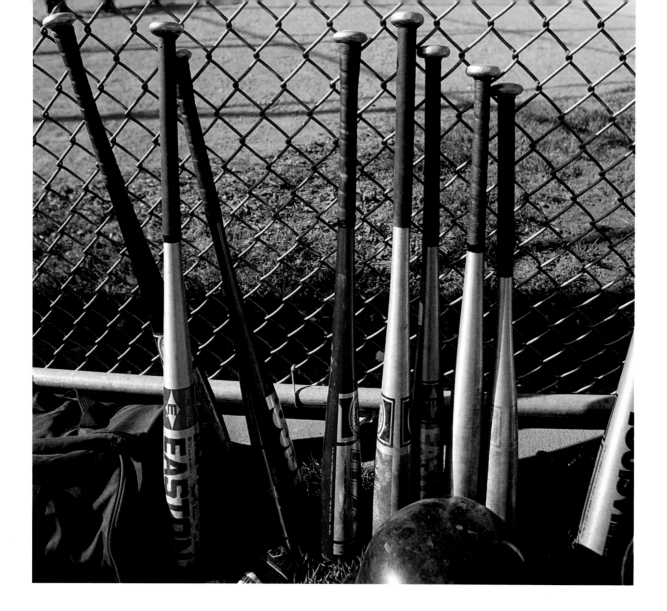

from an old wagon wheel spoke. Aluminum bats are used in youth, high school, and college play because they don't break, but they are illegal in professional baseball. A bat can't be longer than 42 inches and it can't be wider than 2¼ inches at its widest point. The handle of an aluminum bat is covered with a rubber or leather grip and ends in a knob. The portion of the bat that hits the ball is called the barrel.

Choose a light bat that you can swing easily. Most hitters struggle with a bat that is too heavy because they think the heavier the bat, the more power it will generate. Remember, the lighter your bat is, the quicker your swing will be. The quicker your swing, the harder you will hit the ball.

Stretch out your weaker arm at shoulder height. If you can hold the bat level without struggling, it is the correct weight for you. The correct bat length is whatever feels the best when swinging, but the bat should be no more than 3 to 8 inches longer than the number of ounces it weighs. Here are some suggestions:

- ages up to 8 years . . . 15 to 21 ounces
- 9 to 12 years . . . . 21 to 25 ounces
- up to 18 years . . . . . . 25 to 32 ounces

● *The Glove*

You will need to buy a glove that fits the position you most often play. If you are an infielder, choose a small glove so that you can get the ball out of your glove quickly. A pitcher, outfielder, or first baseman needs a larger glove to help scoop up the ball. A catcher needs a special mitt with a padded palm.

When buying a glove, don't just buy the biggest glove or one autographed by your favorite player. Huge gloves can lead to bad habits, like not using your hands properly or not using both hands to catch.

Baseball Gloves

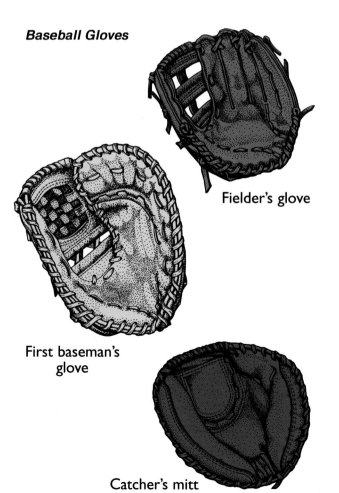

Fielder's glove

First baseman's glove

Catcher's mitt

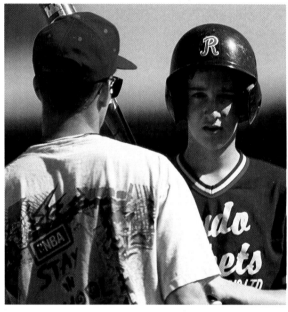

● *Other Equipment*

A baseball player wears a hard plastic cap when batting. This batting helmet protects the batter from a pitched ball while batting and a thrown ball while running the bases. Batting helmets are required in all leagues.

Many baseball players also wear spiked shoes, called cleats, to improve their running. Some also wear a tight-fitting glove, called a batting glove, when they are batting. A batting glove helps these players grip the bat better.

And nearly every baseball player—and even many people who don't play baseball—wears a baseball cap. The wide brim of the cap helps to keep the sun out of a player's eyes.

The Field

A baseball field has an infield, an out-field, and foul territory. The infield is a square area, usually dirt, with a base at each corner. Because the infield looks diamond-shaped from behind home plate, baseball fields are often called *diamonds*.

The outfield is a grassy section between the infield and the fence that borders the field. The size of the outfield varies from field to field.

The infield and outfield are fair territory, which is where the game is played. Foul territory is the area outside the infield and outside the foul lines of the outfield. The foul lines are marked with white chalk. One line extends from each side of home plate to the fence.

● Pitcher's Mound

The pitcher throws the ball from the pitcher's mound, which is 60 feet, 6 inches from home plate. The mound is 18 feet wide and 10 inches high in the center. In the center is a piece of white rubber, 24 inches long and 6 inches wide, known as the rubber. The pitcher's foot must be touching the rubber when he or she releases a pitch.

Outfield

Foul line

Foul territory

Second base

90' (60')

Infield

Third base

Pitcher's mound

Pitching rubber

60' 6" (46')

Home plate

● *The Bases*

First, second, and third bases are white canvas bags filled with sand. The bases are 15 inches square and 5 inches thick. Each base is 90 feet from the next one. After getting a hit, the batter runs to first base, then second base, and then third base. If the batter reaches the fourth base, home plate, a run is scored.

Home plate is a five-sided piece of white rubber. The part of home plate that is nearest the infield is 17 inches wide. Home plate narrows to a point on the side farthest from the infield. The ball is pitched over home plate, and batters stand beside it when taking their swings at the ball. A rectangle, 6 feet by 4 feet, is marked with chalk on each side of home plate. These areas are called the **batter's box**. A batter must be standing in either the left-side or right-side batter's box when the pitch is thrown.

The measurements for Little League play are shown in parentheses ( ).

90' (60')

Foul line

Foul territory

First base

Home Plate Area

Righthanded batter's box

Lefthanded batter's box

Catcher's box

The Rules

A game begins when the pitcher puts his or her foot on the rubber of the pitcher's mound. Then the pitcher throws the ball to the catcher, who crouches behind home plate. The pitcher tries to pitch so that the ball crosses the plate within the **strike zone,** which is an imaginary rectangle from the batter's armpits to his or her knees that is the width of home plate.

A **strike** is called when the batter either swings at the ball and misses or doesn't swing at a pitch that the umpire says was in the strike zone. When three strikes have been called, that batter has made an **out,** called a **strikeout.**

A **ball** is called when the batter doesn't swing at a pitch and the umpire rules that the ball was outside of the strike zone. If four balls are called, the batter is given a **base on balls,** or walk, which means he or she goes to first base.

If the batter swings and hits the ball in fair territory, the batter runs to first base and then keeps running until forced to stop. When the batter hits the ball, the game explodes into action. The batter's **hit** sends fielders sprinting all over the field. If the hit ball is caught in the air, the batter is out. But if the ball isn't caught before it hits the ground, the hitter becomes a baserunner. A baserunner's goal is to touch all the bases, from first base to home plate. Safely reaching home plate records one run for the team at bat. Of course, the team in the field tries to prevent baserunners from reaching base and scoring runs.

Once a baserunner has reached a base, he or she is safe and can't be

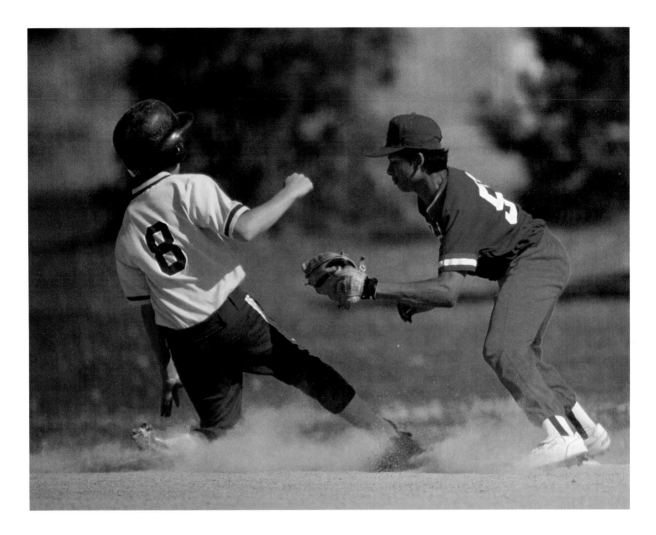

tagged out while still touching the base. The runner can remain on a base until the next batter gets a hit. Once the ball is in play again, the baserunner can continue the challenge of advancing to the next base.

A baserunner is tagged out if he or she isn't on a base and is touched by a fielder who is holding the ball. If a fielder touches a base while holding the ball before the baserunner touches the base, the runner is out if all the bases behind him or her are occupied. This is called a **force-out**. The runner can also be forced out at first base.

If a batter can get to first base safely after hitting the ball, that batter has hit a single. If the batter gets to second base on a hit, that hit is called a double. If the batter reaches third base, the hit is a triple. If the batter reaches home plate on the hit, the batter has hit a **home run**.

If a player hits the ball and a fielder makes a mistake—throws the ball over the first baseman's head, for example—the batter reaches base on an **error**. If a batter hits the ball but reaches first base safely only because the fielders decided to force out a baserunner instead of make the play on the batter, the play is called a **fielder's choice**. If the fielding team puts out two baserunners during one play, the fielders have made a **double play**. Often, a double play is made when a baserunner is on first base and the batter hits the ball to the infield. The fielders can force out the runner at second base and still get the ball to first base before the batter gets there.

Over the past 150 years, baseball has developed some complicated rules to make the game fair. One such rule is the infield fly rule. The rule applies when there are no outs or one out, and at least one runner on base who could be forced out. If the batter hits a **pop-fly** that could be caught by an infielder, the umpire yells "Infield fly. The batter's out!" This prevents a fielder from intentionally dropping the ball in order to make a double play. A baserunner may advance "at his or her own risk" if the ball is dropped.

A baseball game is usually six, seven, or nine innings, depending on the level of play. The visiting team bats first in the game, and each team has one turn at bat with three outs per inning. The exception to this rule is in the last inning, when the home team doesn't bat if it is ahead.

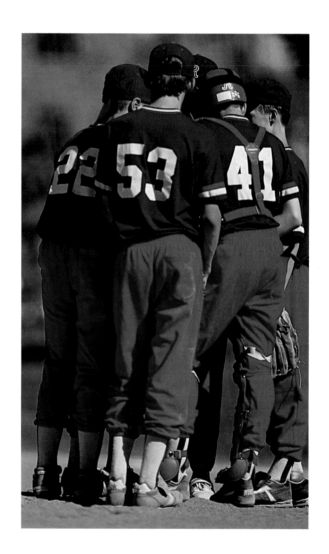

The Positions

Each of the nine fielders has an area of the field for which he or she is responsible. The pitcher is on the pitcher's mound, throwing pitches. The catcher is behind home plate, catching pitches. Together, the pitcher and catcher are called a team's battery.

The first baseman, second baseman, and third baseman all play near their bases. The shortstop plays between the second and third bases. These four players are infielders.

The outfielders are spread across the outfield. The leftfielder is between second and third base. The centerfielder plays behind second base, and the rightfielder is between the first and second bases.

When a team is batting, the players on that team bat in an assigned order, called the **lineup**. The manager decides on the order. The player who is batting is "up." The next player to bat is "on deck," and the player following him or her is "in the hole." Coaches near first base and third base help the baserunners decide when to run.

An umpire calls balls and strikes from behind home plate. The umpire also makes sure the other rules of the game are followed. If there are two or more umpires, the additional umpires are stationed around the bases to rule on whether baserunners are safe or out. If there is only one umpire, he or she must run from behind the plate out into the infield to make base calls.

FIELDING

Baseball is a simple game. There are only four maneuvers a baseball player must be able to do: Field the ball, throw the ball, hit the ball, and run. But baseball isn't an easy game. It will take time and effort to learn how to handle the ball, throw it accurately, hit it, and run efficiently. The best players, in fact, are always improving their skills and learning new ones.

To become a good fielder, learn to catch without a glove. Practice using "soft hands." Soft hands cradle the ball gently, rather than letting the ball slap stiffly against them. Try to catch the ball so that very little sound is heard as it hits your hands. Pretend your hands are glass—if the ball hits your hands too hard, your hands will shatter.

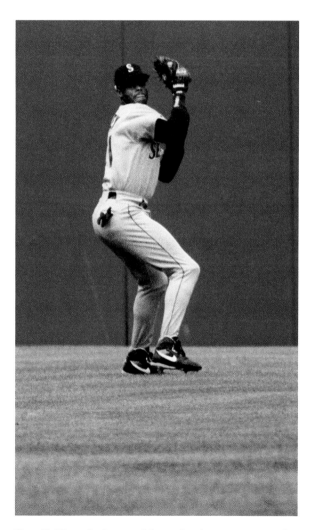

Ken Griffey Jr. began his major league career in the Seattle Mariners' outfield. He was the first American League outfielder to win five straight Gold Gloves.

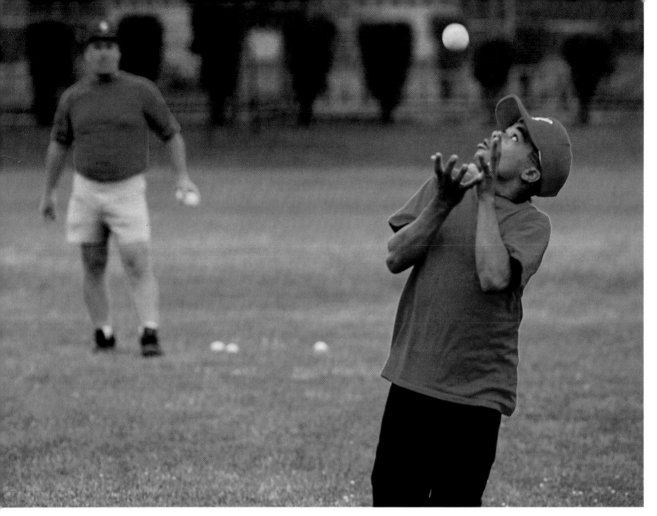

Dave and Andy are practicing a drill also used by football receivers. They use their bare hands and a tennis ball. First, Andy runs five steps away from his coach, who lobs the ball ahead of Andy. Andy looks over his shoulder, finds the ball, and runs to catch it. The coach alternates his throws over Andy's shoulders, first to the left, then the right. Then it's Dave's turn.

After both players have caught 10 balls, they use their gloves and a baseball. Then, Dave runs 10 steps before looking over his shoulder. Dave and Andy remind each other not to reach out with the glove until the last instant before catching the ball. Running with your glove hand extended slows you down and often prevents you from making a great catch.

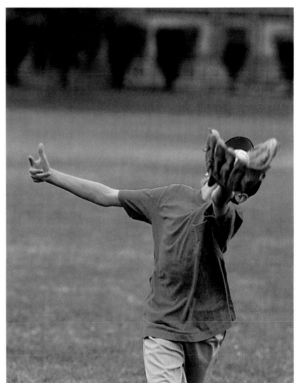

Fielding Ground Balls

Matt and Katy are fielding **ground balls**. Ground balls hit the ground before a fielder can catch them. Because the grass and dirt of the infield is uneven, cleanly fielding ground balls takes patience and practice.

● *The Stance*

As he waits for the batter to hit the ball, Matt's back is bent slightly forward and his hands rest comfortably on his bent knees. He has spread his legs wider than his shoulders to get as low as possible. This gives Matt better balance and enables him to get closer to the ground. He keeps his balance by having his weight on the balls of his feet.

Matt throws with his right hand, so his right foot is slightly behind his left. By having his throwing-side foot slightly back, he is able to throw more quickly.

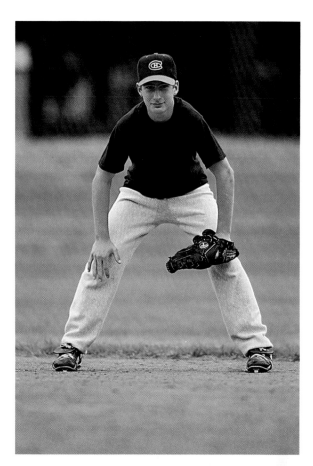

● *The Glove*

Matt has his glove fully open and on the ground, extended forward. Most errors are caused by balls going under the glove, not over it, so keep your glove touching the ground. Extend your arm in front of you so that you can see the ball go into the glove.

Matt's right hand is above the glove. With his glove extended forward, not downward, it can't tangle up Matt's feet. With Matt's hands extended, he can better react to bad hops. His hands can cushion the ball, like shock absorbers. Then he can smoothly bring the ball to the throwing position.

● *Moving to the Ball*

Keep your feet moving when you are fielding a ground ball. Katy charges aggressively to the ball, but then slows down. She gets her body under control to field the ball by spreading her legs to get low. By charging, she reaches the ball quicker and her throw is shorter. Remember, the longer the fielder takes to catch and throw the ball, the more time the baserunner has. Moving forward under control gives you more momentum and a more powerful throw.

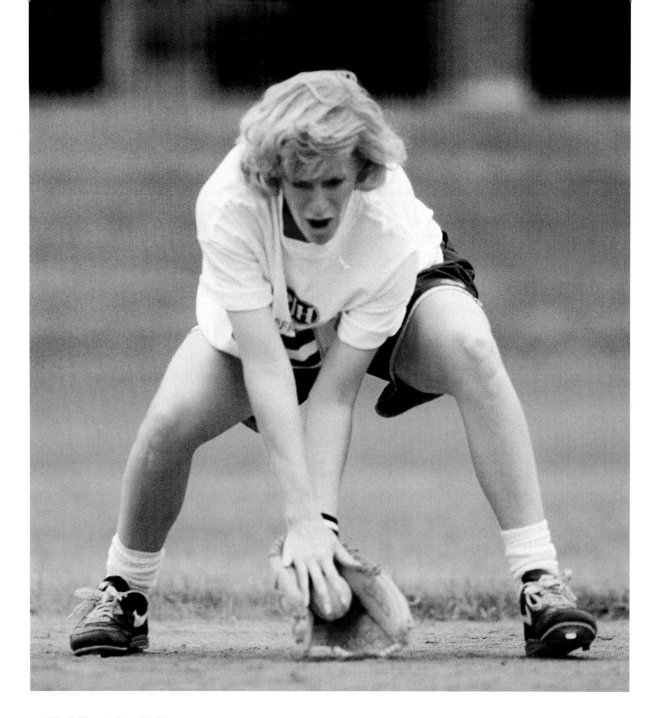

● *Fielding the Ball*

Katy uses both hands to field the grounder. This way, the ball is less likely to pop out of her glove. Watch the ball go into your glove. Even better, try to watch the seams of the ball.

Katy's top hand acts like a garbage can cover. As the ball enters her glove, her throwing hand covers the ball. Using both hands also means Katy will be able to throw the ball more quickly, since her throwing hand is already in contact with the ball.

Use both hands and try to create a fluid motion instead of a two-step action: catch, then throw. Practice doing this in slow motion without a ball until you can imitate your favorite professional infielder's smooth motion.

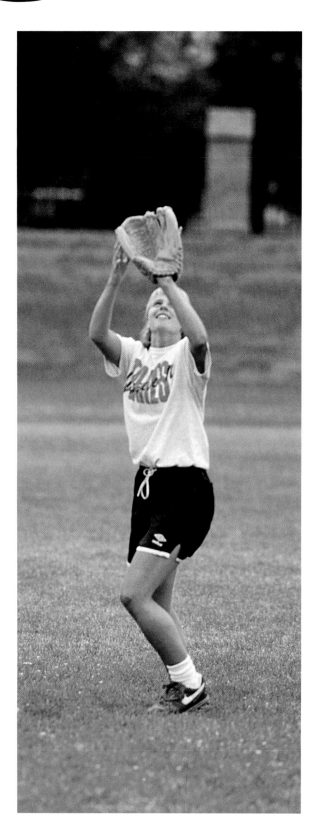

Fielding Fly Balls and Pop-Ups

When catching a **fly ball** or pop-up, remember to use soft hands. Missy is catching a fly ball above her waist, so her gloved fingers are pointed up. Whenever possible, try to catch the ball above your head. That way, your glove can serve as a shield to keep the sun out of your eyes, and you can watch the ball more easily. If you fumble the ball, you have a second try at catching it before it hits the ground. Catching fly balls in your midsection, like some pros do, looks flashy, but you won't have enough time to make a catch if you fumble the ball. And dropping the ball doesn't look flashy.

Trying to catch a ball below your waist with your fingers pointing up is awkward. If you must catch a fly ball below your waist, have your gloved fingers pointing down. Ben is catching a fly ball below his waist. His gloved fingers are pointed down. His bare hand will cover the ball when it is caught.

● *Running to Catch Fly Balls*

Run on the balls of your feet, not your heels, when you must run to catch a fly ball. Running on your heels causes your body to bounce. Running on the balls of your feet cushions your body, and helps keep your vision steady.

Try this: Focus on a fixed object in the air, like the top of a light pole. Run in place, first on your heels, then on the balls of your feet. Notice how much more clearly you can see the light pole's top when you are running on the balls of your feet, rather than on your heels.

THROWING

After fielding the ball, you must make a good throw to complete the play. Learn and use the following fundamentals to focus all of your power toward your target. Be sure your shoulders are level, and that your front shoulder points directly toward your target. Step directly toward that target with your lead foot.

● *The Grip*

A good throw begins with the proper grip. Katy has split her index and middle finger ½ to 1 inch across the baseball's big seams. The pads directly below these fingertips grip the ball loosely. (If your hand is smaller than Katy's, use the next finger also so you grip the ball with three fingers.) Katy's thumb is placed directly underneath and toward the middle of the ball. The

33

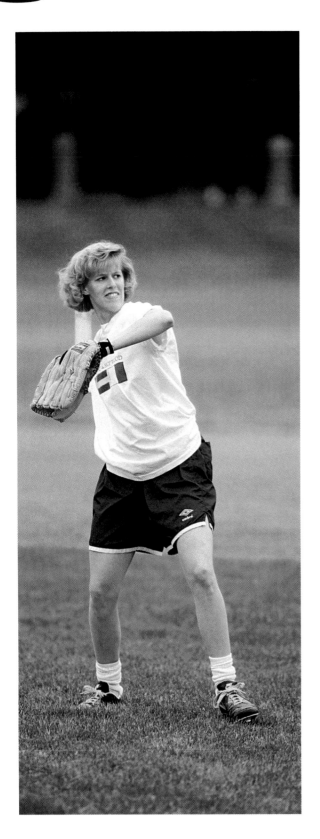

ball rests on the side of the thumb, not the pad of the thumb tip. There is about a half-inch between Katy's palm and the ball.

Hold the ball loosely in your hand for maximum power. From 10 to 20 percent of your throwing power comes from snapping your wrist during the throwing motion. Holding the ball too tightly locks your wrist.

● *The Stance*

Katy's weight is on the ball of her back foot, which is at a 90-degree angle to her target. Katy's back leg is bent, as if she were preparing for a jump shot in basketball. Katy will drive forward off of her back leg toward the target.

Katy's shoulders are level, not sloped toward the sky or the ground. Your front shoulder aims the ball. If your shoulders slope upward, your throw will be a high one. If your shoulders aim to the right or left of the target, the ball will go in that direction.

Katy's glove is at shoulder level, about 12 inches out from her shoulder. Her elbow is down and her wrist is bent. Try thrusting your elbow and glove down naturally toward your front hip. Now cock your throwing arm back in a throwing position and thrust your front elbow and glove downward toward the front hip. Notice how the front side thrusting down also thrusts and rotates the throwing shoulder and arm forward like a whip. This motion generates arm speed.

● Cocking the Arm

After you grip the ball, you must cock your arm for the throw. Katy's arm is behind her. Her palm is down and her elbow is level or slightly above her shoulder. The farther Katy can comfortably extend her arm backward, without her elbow locking, the more power she will generate. This is called the *eagle* position. Think of extending your arm back with the long wingspan of an eagle. If your throws lack speed, your arm is probably only extending back like a duck. Keep the ball just above head height when in this position. If your elbow drops and the ball is below head height, you will push the ball and your throw will be high.

Take Care of Your Arm

A strong arm takes years to develop. If your arm is injured, your baseball career can be crippled. So take care of your arm!

In cool or cold weather, wear a T-shirt, a nylon jacket, and a sweatshirt as minimum protection. You can always take off a layer if you get too hot.

Before throwing, do stretching exercises like toe touches, arm circles, and jumping jacks. Then warm up your muscles by jogging. Start to throw by lobbing the ball half the distance from the plate to the mound. Gradually increase the distance you're throwing until you're throwing from the plate to second base. Easy throwing for five minutes will get you ready.

Don't throw hard or for a long time, especially early in the season. Start slowly and gradually increase your strength. Stop throwing any time your shoulder, elbow, or wrist starts to hurt. If you do develop a sore arm, try resting your arm, doing some extra stretching and running, or hanging from a pull-up bar.

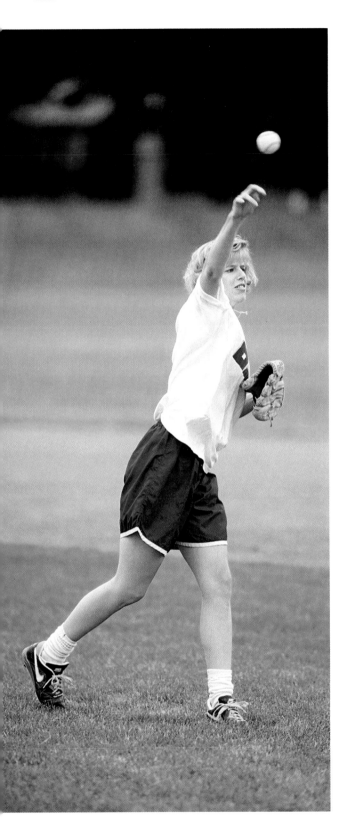

● *The Release*

From this cocking position, Katy shifts most of her weight to her back leg, keeping her shoulders level. Katy's palm has rotated from facing the ground to facing the sky, and her wrist is cocked back. She steps forward 6 to 12 inches directly toward her target with her front foot, landing on the ball of that foot to allow a complete follow through. As she pushes off her back leg and steps toward the target, Katy's front hip rotates so her knee and foot point to the target.

As her front foot hits the ground, her arm thrusts forward. Katy's elbow, level or slightly above her shoulder, leads the thrust as her weight shifts forward, aided by her front side rotating down toward the front hip. Katy whips the ball ahead of her elbow, snapping her wrist, and releases the ball when her arm is fully extended.

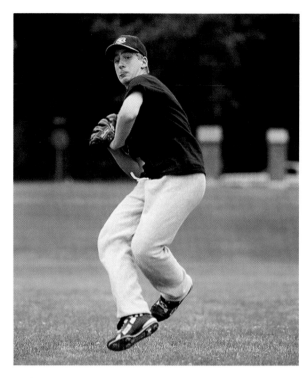

To gain power—for an outfield throw, for example—Matt uses a technique called the *crow hop*. He hops on his back foot with his instep pointing to the target and releases the ball as he steps directly toward the target with his front foot.

● *The Follow-Through*

Katy's throwing hand finishes on the outside of her forward knee. Her back is bent comfortably and her back leg swings forward so that her back foot ends up slightly ahead of her front foot.

Throwing Practice

Practice your throwing motion 25 times a day in slow motion, and you will have a smooth, powerful, and balanced throw. While you practice, be aware of using all your muscles in your feet, legs, sides, back, shoulders, arm, and wrist. The more you use all these muscles, the stronger and healthier your arm will be.

For developing arm strength and endurance, there is no replacement for throwing as much as you can. Play catch with friends anywhere—away from windows, of course!—and as often as possible. Throwing against a wall also helps.

Gradually increase the number and the distance of your throws. If you only throw 90 feet, your arm will never get stronger. Practice throwing by gradually increasing your throwing distance to 125, 150, 175, 200, 225 feet.

Dave and Andy are making high, lazy, long throws, not hard line drives. This strengthens their arms without injuring them. Throw as much and as often as your arm permits. But remember, stop throwing if you feel sore. You only have one good throwing arm. Take care of it!

HITTING

Hitting is the most challenging part of baseball—and the most fun. Don't expect a hit every time. View each **at bat** as a challenge. If you strike out, don't get discouraged. Concentrate on getting a hit the next time. A hitter is considered successful if he or she gets a hit 3 out of every 10 at bats. Successful players learn from mistakes, telling themselves to improve next time.

Hitting seems very complex, but there is only one goal: hit the ball squarely with as quick a swing as possible. Once you have mastered this, you will have a good swing. Then when you enter the batter's box, you will have only two things to think about: selecting a good pitch to hit, and hitting a **line drive** to center field.

Swinging

Practice swinging the bat at imaginary baseballs. (But be sure real lamps aren't nearby!) Get the feel of throwing the barrel quickly and precisely through the ball. Keep practicing this until the bat feels like a natural part of your hands.

● *The Grip*

A good swing requires the correct grip. Dave is holding the bat just above the pads below his fingers with the bottom three fingers of each hand relaxed. Notice how his finger knuckles (those you use when knocking on a door), not his hand knuckles, are lined up. Holding the bat with your fingers and knuckles properly positioned unlocks your wrists for more whip in the swing.

Dave holds the bat firmly, as he would hold a hammer, but not too tightly. Tension is a hitter's enemy. Squeezing the bat too hard slows down your swing and decreases your control.

● *The Ready Position*

Good hitting begins with a solid base. Dave's feet are slightly wider than his shoulders. His weight is on the balls of his feet. He has bent both knees slightly, unlocking his legs' springing power, so that if he looks down he sees his knees but not his feet.

Dave has the bat resting on his shoulder at a 45-degree angle. His top hand is near the top of his rear shoulder. The bat's knob is facing down at his back toe, not toward the catcher. If the knob is facing the catcher, Dave's bat would have a longer path to the ball.

When the pitcher begins the windup, Dave lifts the bat off his shoulder, keeping it at a 45-degree angle. His top hand is even with the top of his back shoulder, over his back toe.

Dave keeps his hands 3 to 5 inches from his body. To understand why, try to hold the bat barrel steady with your hands 8 to 12 inches away from your body while your friend tries to move it. Now try this with your hands closer to your body. You have more strength when your hands are closer to your body. But don't bring your hands too close to your body, or you will not be able to swing freely.

Dave's eyes, shoulders, and elbows are level to ensure good vision and a level swing. If one elbow or one shoulder was higher than the other, Dave's swing would probably be either an uppercut or a downward chop. His front elbow is relaxed. It points down and is toward the front of his body, but not past his belly button. If Dave's front elbow was back too far, his arms would be locked in a more rigid position. That

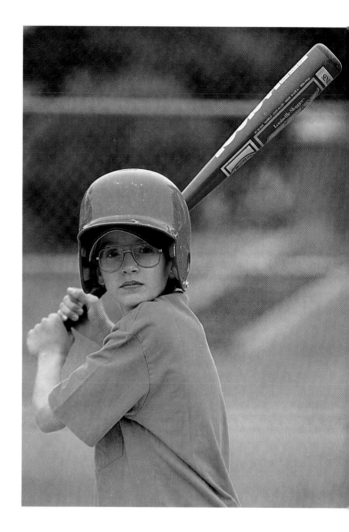

would slow down his swing and make an inside pitch harder for him to hit.

Dave's head is turned so both eyes look directly at the pitcher. His chin is near his front shoulder. (Be sure to turn your head far enough so that your eyes are not blocked by your nose or the bridge of your glasses.) To help you remember what you should do during a swing, think of this position as the *Pete* position. Go from the *Pete* position to the *Sweet* position, in which your chin is near your back shoulder and your eyes are looking down your arms and the bat's barrel, focused on the ball.

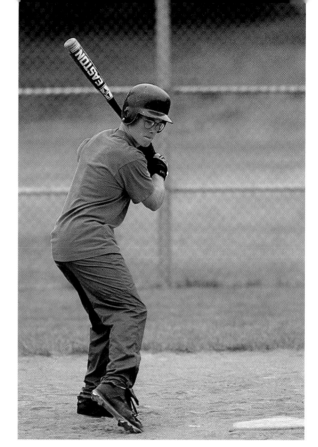

● *Cocking*

To begin the swing, Ben cocks his lower body and hands. When you do this, imagine that your pants have a back pocket on the leg closest to the pitcher. When the pitcher raises his or her leg to pitch, turn your lower body one inch so that the pocket points toward the pitcher. This will cock the front hip and put your weight properly over the back foot.

At the same time Ben cocks his hips, he moves his hands back one or two inches. Imagine a string connecting the hands and hips. As your hip pocket cocks one inch, your hands cock back at the same time.

Keep the bat as still as possible when cocking. The barrel should not be waving back and forth. A still bat is called a quiet bat. A quiet bat begins each swing from the same starting point. Starting from the same spot for each swing results in a consistent swing.

● *Striding*

Next, Ben takes a short, 1- to 3-inch stride forward with his front foot. When striding, your weight will shift from your back leg to your front leg. Your weight should be evenly balanced on both legs after the stride.

Most strides begin as the pitch is released. Ben strides forward simply by lifting his knee about an inch so the front foot is raised onto its ball and the heel is slightly raised. Don't turn this foot so that the toe points to the pitcher. That would rob you of power. Also, Ben strides directly toward the pitcher. A short, balanced stride is key to successful hitting.

Ben lands on the ball of his front foot and, as his swing continues, he shifts his weight to his heel. When striding, imagine that you are stepping onto a thin piece of ice. Stepping too hard would send you crashing into the water.

● *The "Sweet" Position*

When the bat hits the ball, Ben is looking down his arms and the barrel of the bat. His eyes are focused on the ball. His chin is near his back shoulder and his upper body and chest are balanced, not leaning over the plate. His back elbow is close to his body but his arms are almost fully extended. Remember, this is sometimes called the *Sweet* position. You go from *Pete* to *Sweet* when swinging properly.

Ben's hips have rotated to release his lower body's power, like a giant spring uncoiling. His back foot has pivoted 90 degrees, so his toe is pointing toward the pitcher. This motion is like squishing a bug. The player who doesn't squish the bug isn't releasing all of his or her power. The point at which the bat contacts the ball is slightly ahead of Ben's body, where his bat speed is the fastest. Ben's bottom hand and left elbow pull down and directly toward the pitcher while his top hand throws the barrel of the bat toward and through the ball. Think of driving the knob of the bat downward and directly toward the pitcher. Meanwhile, Ben's top arm extends at contact.

By thrusting his hands toward the pitcher and throwing the barrel ahead of his hands and through the ball, Ben has a quick, compact swing. When you are swinging, keep your hands close to your body and concentrate on whipping the barrel through the ball.

Practice = Perfection

After you have learned the fundamentals of hitting, there is only one way for you to become a better hitter. You must practice, and practice correctly. Practice doesn't necessarily make perfect, practice makes permanent. So with every swing, practice perfectly so perfection becomes permanent. A Chinese proverb explains: "Hear it, you forget; see it, you understand; do it, you learn; practice it, you become perfect."

By practicing and thinking about the quickest path to the ball, your mind will train your body so the action will become automatic. Start with this practice routine:

1. Each day choose one or two parts of the swing to improve.

2. Swing 25 times in slow motion.

3. Then take 25 good swings, thinking about the part of the swing you're working on. A good practice swing is not just waving a bat in the air. Imagine yourself in a real game. Visualize yourself hitting pitches in all parts of the strike zone. Feel confident. Feel relaxed.

4. Next, hit 25 balls off of a tee, like Don Mattingly and Wade Boggs do. You can use whiffle balls or tennis balls.

● *Following Through*

As Ben follows through, he keeps his head still and his eyes focused on the point of contact. Train your head and eyes to stay down and focused on the contact point even after you have hit the ball. You will see and hit the ball more consistently. Your hands should finish up near your front shoulder.

Release your top hand after contact if that's comfortable for you. Some people believe that the top hand must be released. Great hitters have been successful, however, keeping both hands on the bat. The key to success is doing what works best for you.

The Mental Game

You may have the world's best swing, but if you lack confidence, swing at pitches over your head or in the dirt, or don't use the whole field in hitting, you will not be consistently successful.

Develop a positive attitude. Practice daily, by yourself and with friends, and you will improve. Set realistic goals. Try to get on base once a game with a walk, error, or hit. Once you reach this goal, every other time you get on base is a bonus.

While you are sitting in the dugout during a game, study the other team's pitcher. Try to learn that pitcher's patterns. Are this pitcher's pitches usually high or low? What pitches does this pitcher throw in different situations—starting a batter, when ahead in the count, and when behind in the count?

Next, have a plan at the plate. Be selective, but be aggressive. Attack every good pitch. Don't swing at pitches you don't like. Don't worry about your mechanics. Work on improving your mechanics at practice, not at the plate.

Focus on the pitcher's release point and try to see the seams of the ball spin. Try to see the ball hit your bat, and practice keeping your head down at the contact point until your follow-through is completed.

Study the pitcher's grip, the release point, and the spin of the ball to distinguish a **fastball**, a **change-up**, or a **curveball**. If the pitcher falls behind in

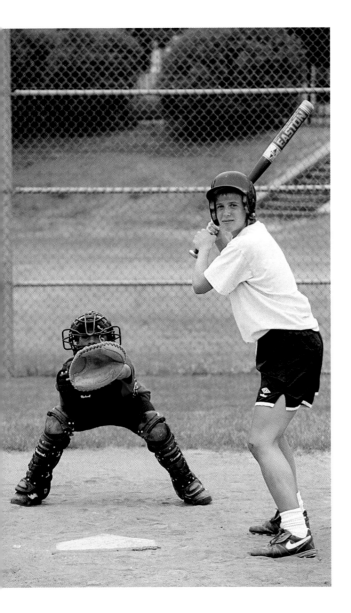

the count by throwing balls, you can be choosy. Before you have a strike against you, look for the pitch that you can hit best. Your best pitch may be high or low, to the inside or to the outside part of the plate. Always look for a fastball toward the middle of the plate when you have an advantage in the count.

With one strike, you can't be as picky. Look for a pitch you can drive, even if it's not in your favorite spot. With two strikes, focus on hitting the ball somewhere. Be aggressive—don't let the umpire's call determine your success. An umpire's strike zone may be inconsistent, so put the ball in play and make the other team put you out.

● Hitting Line Drives

To raise your **batting average,** focus on hitting a line drive over the pitcher's head on every pitch. Why? Hitting up the middle gives you more chances to find an open spot. If your timing is correct, the ball will be a single up the middle. If your swing is just a little early or late, the single could become an extra-base hit to left or right field.

Also, the middle is the most open area of the field. The shortstop and second baseman are on either side of second base. The pitcher is often off balance after releasing the ball. A hard-hit ball up the middle gives the pitcher and infielders little time to react and field the ball cleanly.

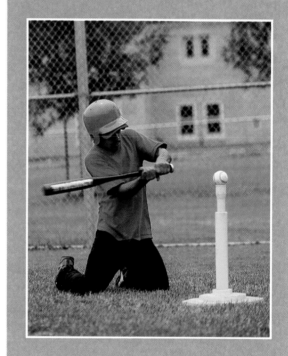

Whole-Body Hitting

The best hitters use all their muscles to hit. Your legs, hips, and back muscles are much stronger than just your arms and hands. To prove this to yourself or a friend, get on your knees and try to swing. Notice how little power is generated by the arms alone. Use your entire body when hitting.

● Hitting to All Fields

Being able to hit the ball where you want to is called hitting to all fields. Doing that depends on where the ball is in relation to your body when you hit it.

To *pull* the ball means to hit it to left field if you are a righthanded hitter, or right field if you are lefthanded. To pull the ball, Ben hits it farther in front of his body. To hit to center field, Ben hits the ball slightly in front of his body with the barrel slightly ahead of his wrists. To hit the ball to the opposite field (right field for a righthander), Ben hits the ball when it is even or slightly behind the midpoint of his body.

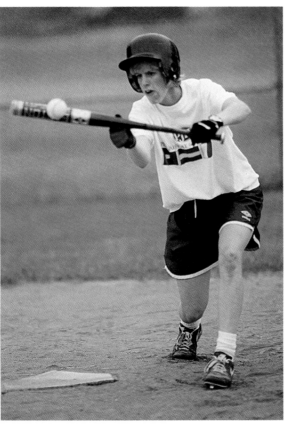

● Bunting

Bunting—softly tapping a pitch so that it drops on the infield grass—can cause more confusion and opportunities than any other play in baseball. And bunting also improves hitting. Learning to bunt develops your timing and helps you to see the ball better. With practice, anyone can become an excellent bunter. The following steps explain a **sacrifice** bunt where the main goal is to advance a runner, not for the batter to get on base. However, a good bunt often gets you on base.

Bunting begins with a good soft grip, as Katy illustrates. Take your back hand and make an imaginary squirt gun, with your thumb extended upward and your index finger pointed outward as the gun barrel. Now, pull your index finger as if you were pulling the trigger so your finger is curled inward. You have made a V with the base of the thumb and the fleshy area that extends to the fingers. The bat should rest loosely in the V. Your fingers and thumb are protected behind the surface of the bat, not wrapped around it.

Loosely grip the handle of the bat with your other hand's fingers wrapped around the handle. This hand should be 12 to 18 inches from the knob. The bat's barrel should slant upward and be close to eye level so you can watch the ball hit the bat. Also, keep the bat higher than the ball to avoid popping up. Move forward in the batter's box so the bat is in fair territory. This increases your chances of a fair, not foul, bunt. A foul bunt is a strike. Remember, if you have two strikes and you hit a foul bunt, you are out.

There are two stances for bunting: the pivot or the square-off. In both stances, the batter's knees are bent so that his or her strike zone is lower.

The pivot stance is the easiest method. The hitter stands a little closer to the plate and pivots on the balls of his or her feet until his or her hips face the pitcher.

In the square-off stance, the batter steps away from the plate with his or her front foot until it is parallel with his or her back foot and with the side of the batter's box. Both hips face the pitcher and the feet are spread wider than shoulder-width apart.

Ben holds the bat's barrel at the top of the strike zone and over the entire width of the plate. He moves his bat in just one direction—down. He brings the bat to the ball by bending his knees and lowering his body, not his hands. He lets the ball come to the bat. Think of "catching" the ball with the bat.

To practice bunting, pick out a couple of letters from the brand name on your bat, 3 or 4 inches from the end of the bat. Try to see the ball hit those letters on your bat when you bunt.

If you want to bunt the ball to the same side of home plate as you are standing, point the barrel of the bat in that direction by moving your back hand forward. If you want to bunt to the opposite side, move the back hand back.

Bunting is fun to practice. Have a friend stand 10 to 20 feet away from you. Put a target where each baseline would be. Have your friend toss you a soft pitch and try to bunt it to one of the targets. Switch positions after every 10 pitches.

BASERUNNING

Aggressive baserunning changes a predictable game into a game of chance and daring. To be a good baserunner, you must first be a good runner. Start with a relaxed body. Tight muscles will reduce your speed. Keep your feet pointed straight ahead and explode off the balls of your feet with your knees pumping almost to your waist and your heels kicking back to your buttocks. Pump your arms along the sides of your body, not across it. Your hands should pump to eye level.

● *Running After a Hit*

When you have mastered good running form, concentrate on these two principles of baserunning: always run as fast as you can, and be as aggressive as possible. When you run at top speed, you force the fielders to make their play cleanly and without delay. Fielders are more apt to make a mistake if they are worrying about you hustling down to first. If the fielders do make a mistake or hesitate, be ready to take an extra base.

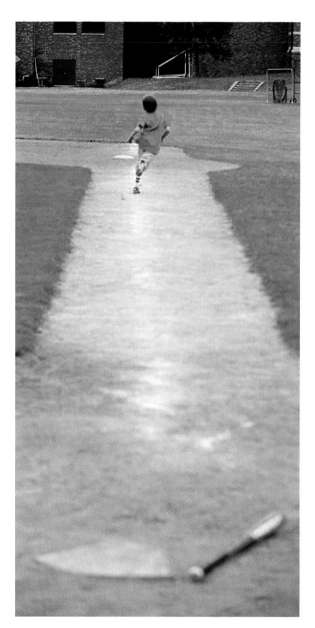

Baserunning begins at home plate. After Dave hits the ball, he drops his bat after following through. Don't take any steps while holding the bat—it's just extra weight that will slow you down. Dave sprints down the first baseline until he gets halfway to first base. Then he makes sure he is running in foul territory (to the right of the line). If a fielder's throw hits Dave while he is in fair territory, the umpire will call him out for interference.

Dave runs two or three steps past first base before slowing down, just in case he can take advantage of a misplay and go to second base. If Dave turns toward second base, the fielders may try to tag him out even though he

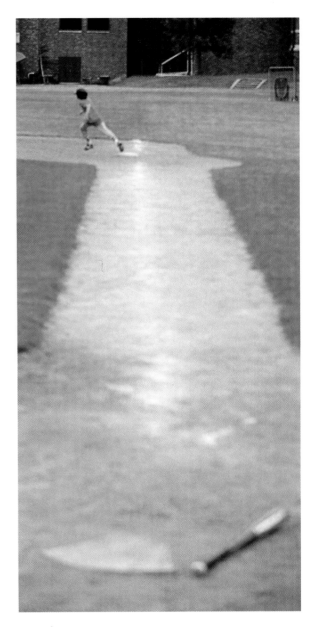

has already touched first base. But if Dave turns toward foul territory to return to first base, he's entitled to safely return to the base.

If Dave's hit reaches the outfield, his goal is second base. He sprints to first base, but rounds the base by veering to his right 4 to 6 feet when he is two-thirds of the way there. He touches first

base with his right foot and pushes off the bag toward second.

Round the bag with as tight a turn as possible so that your first step after touching first base takes you directly toward second base. Don't take too wide a turn before or after touching first base. Use this tight-turn technique when running all the bases.

● *Leading Off*

An aggressive lead gives a baserunner the best possible chance of advancing to the next base, either on a hit or a **stolen base**. When leading off, always watch the pitcher, not your feet. You want to be as far off the base as possible, usually 10 to 15 feet, without getting put out.

Don't jump off the base when leading off. Ben has his right toe on the corner of first base and is facing second base. He takes a 2-foot step with his left foot and then a 2-foot step with his right foot. Ben turns and faces home plate before taking two 2½-foot shuffle steps toward second base. Don't cross your feet. Have your weight on the balls of your feet and keep your body fairly upright and relaxed.

Ben's first movement to the next base is to throw his left arm across his body as he pivots on his right foot. Then he uses good running form.

Another good technique is the walking lead. Walk toward the next base as the pitcher releases the ball. As the ball crosses home plate, stop but lean toward the next base. Then, if the pitch gets past the catcher or is hit, you have a head start.

Ben, the baserunner, is as far from second base as is the closest fielder—in this case, Dave, the second baseman.

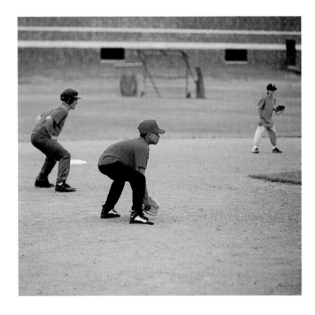

When you are on second base, you can lead off as far as the shortstop and second baseman are from the bag. For example, the closest fielder, Dave, is 15 feet from the bag, so Ben is leading off about 15 feet. Try to lead off 5 feet behind a straight line from second base to third base. This helps you watch the second baseman and shortstop. Also, if there's a hit, you are in position to round third base and sprint for home.

A good trick is to take an extra-long lead and dare the catcher to pick you off of second base. As the catcher releases the ball, sprint to third. You will be on third before the fielder can catch the ball and throw to the third baseman.

When you're on second base, don't run when any ball is hit to your right unless there's a runner on first or you are positive that the ball will reach the outfield. If the ball is hit to the area between the shortstop and third baseman, the shortstop could field the ball and make a short, quick throw to third for an easy out. But, if the ball is hit to your left, sprint for third base. The fielder will have to field the ball and throw across the infield.

When leading off third base, as Missy is, stand 2 feet in foul territory and as far from the bag as the third baseman is positioned. If a batted ball hit Missy while she was in foul territory, she wouldn't be out. But if she was in fair territory (on the baseline or on the second-base side of it) when she was hit by a batted ball, she would be out.

As the pitch is released, Missy takes two steps toward home plate and leans forward. She's ready to sprint home if the ball gets past the catcher or if it's hit.

● *Stealing*

To **steal** a base, a baserunner must watch the pitcher. If you want to see a pitcher's **pickoff move,** just take a slightly longer lead to draw a throw. Be ready to rush back to the base on the pitcher's first move. Once you know the pitcher's move, you're better prepared to steal.

When a righthanded pitcher raises his or her front foot in order to throw a pitch, the baserunner can start for the next base. A lefthander could step toward first base. If the pitcher steps off the rubber with his or her back foot, the pitcher cannot throw a pitch and is likely to throw to a base.

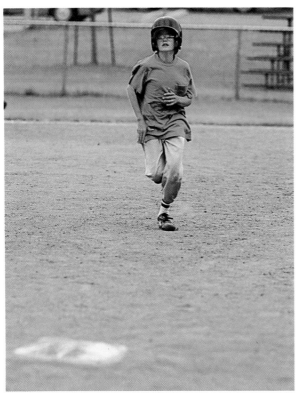

● *Sliding*

When you are a baserunner, sooner or later you will need to **slide**. Sliding into a base in a big cloud of dust is a lot of fun. Aside from having fun, sliding is helpful when you're trying to avoid being tagged, running into a fielder, or overrunning a base. Wear long, heavy pants when you're learning to slide and practice in stocking feet on the grass.

Dave starts his slide when he's about 10 feet from the base. He lifts both feet from the ground at the same time. Don't hop into the slide—glide into it. Dave extends his right leg to the base and bends his left leg. He turns his left foot out to the side so his spikes don't catch in the dirt.

Dave raises his arms above and behind his head. He touches the base with his left foot. He pushes off with his right foot to boost himself upright. Then he can quickly go on to third base if there was an error on the play.

ON THE FIELD

Baseball's nine positions each require special physical and mental skills, but catching, throwing, and running fundamentals are used at all the positions. You also need concentration, good work habits, judgment, and confidence to be successful.

Work on developing skills, but have fun. You will improve. After you have practiced the fundamentals, you'll want to use those skills in a game. College coach Lefty Cyson once said, "You can't play well unless you're relaxed. So relax! You can't be relaxed unless you're having fun. So go out and have fun!" Don't let anyone—fans, parents, coaches, teammates, or opponents—wreck your fun.

Pitcher

Pitching has been called 70 to 90 percent of the game. Good pitching gives your team the chance to win every game. Besides a strong and accurate throwing arm, confidence is the most important ingredient in a pitcher.

As a pitcher, you will have discouraging days. Sometimes you will walk many batters. You may be called for a **balk**. Bad hops, rain, or wind may be factors in losing games. Great pitches may be called balls by umpires or turned into game-winning hits by opponents.

Teammates, opposing players, and fans can all add pressure to your pitching. But remember—the only real pressure you have is the pressure you put on yourself. Concentrate on hitting the catcher's glove. Don't listen to anyone's distracting voice. Have confidence that with dedication and hard work you will be successful. Have fun on the mound! See each pitching appearance as a challenge and opportunity to improve.

To become a good pitcher, there are four basic body positions to learn. All

the motions require balance. Practice these motions in front of a mirror. Soon you will master even the positions that are uncomfortable at first. When you watch major league games, notice how deliberately and slowly the pitchers move until they are about to release the ball. This slowness helps the pitcher stay balanced.

Jay will demonstrate these positions. He's lefthanded. If you're not, just pretend you are looking in a mirror and use the opposite hand or foot that Jay is using. Jay starts with his feet shoulder-width apart. His front foot is 6 inches toward the first baseline. He keeps the ball hidden in his glove. The glove is held at chest level.

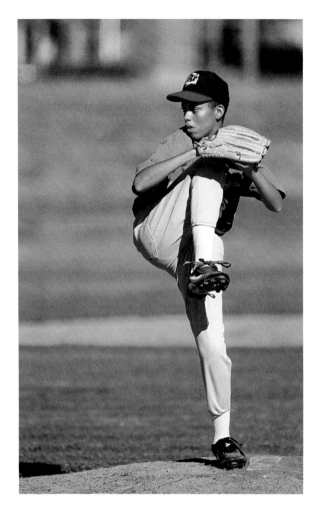

his palm is facing down, his hand is above head height and his elbow is above his shoulder. When Jay whips the ball forward and downward from this position, gravity helps accelerate the ball. Jay reaches back comfortably, his elbow is bent slightly. This coiling of his arm creates more power.

Jay's upper body can supply him with extra power. Think about Dracula raising his cape to hide his fangs. Jay uses that motion with his glove arm as his other arm is lifting the ball. Jay lifts the glove about 10 inches away from his front shoulder. His elbow is down and his glove wrist is bent loosely.

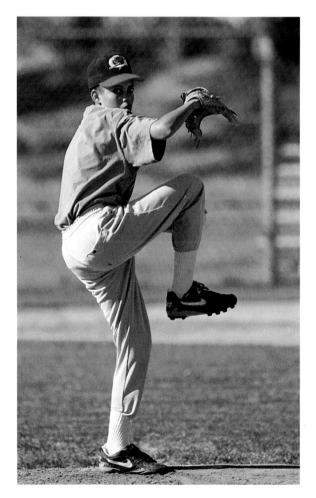

● *Knee to Glove*

Jay lifts his front knee above his waist so that his glove is a few inches above his knee. His weight is on the ball of his back foot. His knee is bent, as if he were going to jump. Think of your knee and its foot as a puppet's. When you lift your knee, keep your foot directly underneath it. When your foot is directly below your knee, your body is balanced. Balance is the key concept. Being balanced gives your body its maximum power.

● *Eagle to Dracula*

After Jay brings his glove above his knee, he takes the ball out of the glove into the eagle position. In this position,

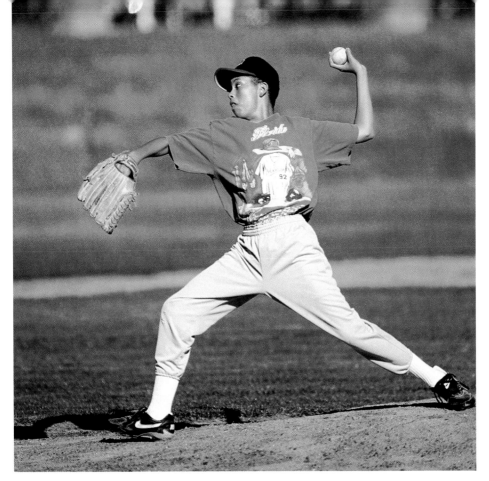

● Pull to Throw

Now Jay is poised to throw. He pulls his front elbow down toward his hip as he cocks his throwing wrist so that the fingers are on top of the ball and his palm is facing upward.

As he pulls down his front elbow, Jay steps forward on his front leg. He lands on the ball of his front foot. His front foot points directly toward home plate. By using his whole body to throw, Jay protects his arm muscles and generates more power.

As Jay's back leg pushes forward, the front of his body pulls his arm forward. His wrist whips the ball directly toward the catcher's mitt. He releases the ball when it is 2 to 3 feet in front of his body, at about the level of his hat. The toe of his front foot points directly toward the catcher's mitt.

● *Follow-Through*

Jay continues to push off his back leg. As his front side pulls him forward and down, he shifts his weight so that he finishes with the back foot even with or slightly ahead of the front foot. Meanwhile, his throwing arm continues to its full extension. His throwing hand finishes near his opposite knee. After completing his follow-through, Jay gets into a ready position so that he can field any ball hit his way.

Throwing Across Your Body

Throwing across your body can hurt your throwing shoulder. If your front foot steps across your body, it prevents your hips and front side from rotating fully. For a right-handed thrower, this means the front foot lands to the right of an imaginary line from the front shoulder to the target. For a left-hander, this means the front foot lands to the left of a line from the front shoulder to the left of the target.

To avoid throwing across your body, make a line in the dirt or tape a straight line on the floor directly toward your target. Then check where your foot lands. It should land on the line or tape to ensure the correct, direct step to the target. This simple test can help keep your arm strong and healthy.

Catcher

A catcher must be tough, alert, have a strong arm, and a good understanding of baseball. A catcher also must not mind being hit by the ball, or by incoming baserunners. Foul tips and wild pitches assault catchers regularly. Dramatic slides home usually mean contact between a sliding baserunner and the catcher.

A catcher often tells the pitcher what pitch to throw and where, using hand signals. To do this, Andy squats with his buttocks on his heels. His back is straight and his glove rests on his left knee to block the third base coach's view. Andy's right hand is between his legs. Using his fingers, he signals to the pitcher which pitch to throw.

When there is a runner on base, the catcher must be able to quickly throw the ball after a pitch. Andy spreads his legs a little wider and extends his glove toward the pitcher. His throwing hand is behind his back or the glove. After catching the ball, Andy brings it back to the eagle position as if drawing back a spear. At the same time, he steps directly toward the target.

Catchers must also block balls that are thrown in the dirt. To do this, Andy falls to his knees with his glove on the ground, blocking the space between his knees. He hunches forward with his shoulders and tucks his chin. He doesn't have to catch the ball—just keep it in front of him.

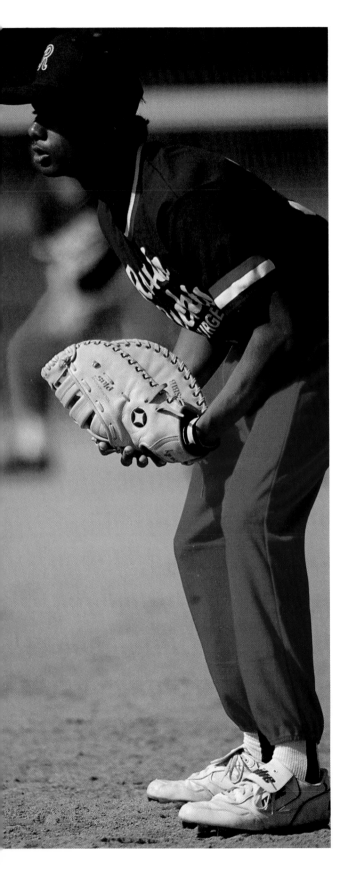

First Base

A first baseman must be able to catch all types of throws and cover the bag. This player doesn't have to be fast or have great range, but being tall is helpful when a fielder's throw is high.

To catch any throw, the first baseman must sprint to the bag as soon as the hitter makes contact. The first baseman places a foot on the front of the bag and faces the fielder who is making the play. The first baseman keeps his or her foot on the bag and stretches as far as possible to receive the ball as quickly as possible.

Perhaps the most difficult play for a first baseman is catching a throw in the dirt. Be sure your glove is on the ground and extended outward so your elbow is almost straight. Pretend that your glove is made of glass. If the ball hits it too hard, the glove will break. Keep your body loose and "give" with the ball to soften the ball's impact. Watch the ball go into your glove.

Second Base

A second baseman can be tall or short, fat or skinny, strong or weak. But a second baseman needs to have quick feet, good hands, and a quick release. Many games are won or lost by a play involving the second baseman. A second baseman must be able to complete a double play, cover first base on a bunt, and handle popups.

Two of the most important plays a second baseman must make are tagging the runner and turning a double play. To tag a baserunner, the second baseman must sprint to the bag and present a good target for the throw.

Straddle the bag. After you catch the ball, sweep your glove down and tag the bag. This way, the runner tags him or herself out trying to touch the base. If you reach out for the runner, he or she may slide underneath or around your tag. Apply the tag with both hands. Have your throwing hand inside the glove, holding the ball.

● Double Play

The footwork for turning a double play is perhaps the most graceful movement in baseball. If the ball is hit to the third-base side of second base, the second baseman sprints to the bag and straddles it to receive the throw. Once the second baseman has the ball, that player must square his or her shoulders and face directly toward first base while throwing the ball to the first baseman. If the ball is hit to the first-base side of second base, the second baseman fields the ball and the shortstop covers second base.

There are two ways to avoid a sliding baserunner and make the throw to first base. In the catch-and-rock-back method, touch the bag with your left foot and have your right foot about 2 feet from the bag. As you catch the ball, rock back to the right foot, then push off and throw to first. In the catch-and-drag method, touch the bag with your right foot, keeping your left foot behind the bag. As you catch the ball, drag your left foot across the bag, push off with your right, and throw the ball.

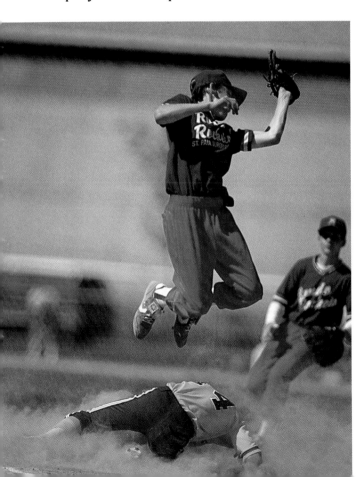

Wall Ball

Here's how to practice your fielding and throwing form. Find a flat, fairly smooth surface leading up to a wall, sturdy garage door, or steps. With a tennis or rubber ball, practice throwing the ball against this surface. When working out against the wall, remember to get low by spreading your feet wider than your shoulders. Also, keep your throwing-side foot slightly behind your other foot.

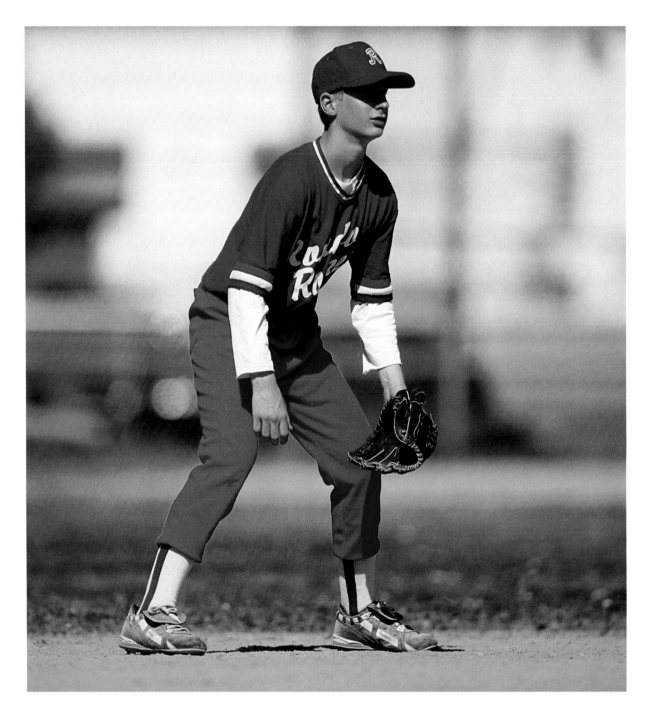

Shortstop

A shortstop needs quickness, range, confidence, good hands, and a strong, accurate throwing arm. A shortstop must field the ball, back up other fielders, and direct outfielders on where to throw the ball. Because the shortstop has so much ground to cover, he or she must be able to anticipate a play.

Third Base

The third baseman needs good hands and a strong arm. A common play for a third baseman is to field a bunt down the third baseline. The third baseman must charge the ball, field it cleanly, and throw it quickly and accurately.

The third baseman must run full-speed to the ball. When he or she reaches it, the third baseman spreads his or her legs and crouches down to field the ball. If the ball is not moving, the third baseman can pick it up with his or her bare hand. If the ball is moving, the third baseman should catch it with his or her glove and both hands. Catch the ball with the left foot forward. Then, still crouched, step forward on the right foot and throw. Don't take any more steps. Any extra step by the fielder means two or three by the baserunner.

Hitting the Cutoff

A cutoff is any fielder who receives a throw with the intention of relaying the ball to another fielder. Here's an example that is illustrated in the diagram below:

With a runner on second base, Willie lashes a double to the left-center field fence. Jeremy, the center fielder, runs to field the ball as the shortstop, Ernie, runs halfway out into the outfield. Jeremy throws the ball to Ernie. Ernie catches the ball, turns, and whips a throw to the third baseman, Mike, who is halfway between home plate and Ernie. Mike catches the ball, turns, and throws to the catcher, Brad, who catches the ball, and tags out the runner who had been on second base. Ernie and Mike were the cutoffs in the play.

The cutoff player should be in a direct line between the fielder and the ultimate target. Because the fielder is concentrating on fielding the ball, the cutoff should yell to the fielder and give him or her a clear target.

To be effective, the cutoff has to consider the strength of the fielder's arm and the distance of the throw. The cutoff must adjust to the fielder's arm strength and move close enough to ensure a good throw that will reach the cutoff at chest height.

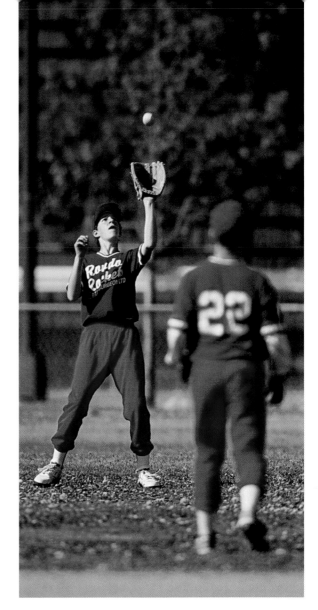

Outfield

All outfielders need to be able to catch fly balls and make long, accurate throws. Good outfielders use the crow hop to make powerful throws in one continuous motion.

A centerfielder should be the fastest outfielder, because he or she has the most ground to cover. A rightfielder should have the strongest arm, because the longest throw an outfielder must make is the throw from right field to third base. A leftfielder must be the most reliable fielder, since most balls hit to the outfield will be hit to left field.

Learning to play baseball gives you something in common with millions of people who learned the game as children. They grew up playing and watching it and passed their love of the game onto their children.

Although baseball is sometimes called America's game, it is, in fact, a popular sport in many countries throughout the world. Whether you are playing baseball inside a building on artificial grass with a synthetic ball and an aluminum bat, or outside at a park on gravel with a taped-up ball and a broom handle for a bat, baseball is a great game!

BASEBALL TALK

at bat: An official attempt to hit a pitched ball. Hitting a sacrifice, being walked, or being hit by a pitch doesn't count as an at bat.

balk: An illegal motion by the pitcher when there is at least one runner on base. If the pitcher is called for a balk, the runner or runners advance one base. The three most common ways to balk are dropping the ball while touching the rubber, not coming to a full stop before throwing a pitch, and stopping the delivery motion before releasing the ball.

ball: A pitch that doesn't pass through the strike zone and at which the batter doesn't swing.

base on balls: A free pass to first base, awarded to a batter who receives four balls before being put out by a strikeout or a fielder. Also called a walk.

batter's box: One of two 4 foot by 6 foot rectangles, 6 inches from both sides of home plate. The batter's boxes are marked with chalk. The batter must have one foot in one of the boxes when hitting the ball.

batting average: The number of hits a batter gets, divided by his or her official at bats (not counting walks or sacrifices), carried to three decimal places. For example, if Dave has 9 at bats and gets 3 hits, his batting average is .333— excellent!

change-up: An intentionally slow pitch that is thrown with the same motion as a fastball to fool the hitter.

curveball: A pitch thrown with a snap and twist of the pitcher's wrist. A right-handed pitcher's curve breaks from right to left; a left-hander's breaks from left to right.

double play: The act of putting out two baserunners on one play in a continuous sequence. One of the most common double plays occurs when the batter hits the ball to the second baseman when there is a runner on first. The second baseman or shortstop forces out the runner at second and throws to first to put out the batter.

error: A mistake by a fielder that results in a batter or baserunner reaching a base safely.

fastball: A pitch thrown at full speed.

fielder's choice: A decision by a fielder who has fielded a batted ball, to throw the ball to a base other than first base in order to put out a runner already on base. The batter isn't credited with a hit even if the play isn't successful.

fly ball: A batted ball that goes high into the air above fair territory.

force-out: A situation in which a baserunner must go to the next base, but the fielder holding the ball touches the base before the baserunner. A force-out, also called a force play, can only happen at first base or when there is a runner on first base.

ground ball: A batted ball that rolls or bounces on the ground. Also called a grounder.

hit: A batted ball that causes the batter to reach base safely without benefit of an error, fielder's choice, or interference call.

home run: A batted ball that goes over the fence in fair territory to score a run for the batter's team once he or she touches all the bases. Any runners on base when the ball is hit also score. If there are three runners on base when a home run is hit, it's called a grand slam home run. An inside-the-park home run is a batted ball that is hit to such a place that the base-runner can touch all the bases before the ball is thrown home. Also called a homer.

inning: A division of the game in which each team has a turn to bat.

line drive: A hard-hit ball that travels on a straight, relatively low path.

lineup: The order in which the members of a team bat. Once the game has started, the lineup can't be changed, although substitutions are allowed. Also called the batting order.

out: The failure of a batter to reach a base safely. A team is allowed three outs in an inning.

pickoff move: A sudden throw from the pitcher or catcher to an infielder to catch a baserunner off base.

pop fly: A batted ball that goes high in the air above the infield.

putout: A play in which a defensive player stops or catches the ball to cause a batter or runner to be out.

sacrifice: A play in which the batter hits the ball and is put out but succeeds in advancing a team-mate at least one base. The batter's team must have fewer than two outs.

slide: The action of a baserunner who, to avoid over-running the base or being tagged out, drops to the ground and slides to the base.

stolen base: A base that a baserunner reaches without the benefit of a hit, error, or fielder's choice.

strike: A pitch that passes through the strike zone without being hit. Also, a pitch that is hit foul when the batter has fewer than two strikes. A foul bunt is also a strike.

strikeout: An out resulting from a batter being charged with three strikes.

strike zone: The area over home plate between the batter's armpits and the top of the knees. The pitch must pass through this zone to be a strike, unless the batter swings and misses.

tag: The action of a fielder in touching a baserunner with the ball in order to put out the baserunner.

FURTHER READING

Galt, Margot Fortunato. *Up to the Plate, The All American Girls Professional Baseball League.* Minneapolis, Minn.: Lerner Publications, 1995.

Jordon, Pat. *Sports Illustrated Pitching: The Keys to Excellence.* New York: Sports Illustrated Books, 1988.

Kindall, Jerry. *Sports Illustrated Baseball: Play the Winning Way.* Lanham, Maryland: Sports Illustrated Books, 1993.

Schmidt, Mike, and Rob Ellis. *The Mike Schmidt Study: Hitting Theory, Skills and Technique.* New York: McGriff & Bell, 1994.

Winfield, Dave, with Eric Swenson. *The Complete Baseball Player.* New York: Avon Books, 1990.

FOR MORE INFORMATION

Babe Ruth Baseball
524½ Hamilton Avenue
Trenton, N.J. 08609

Little League Baseball, Inc.
P.O. Box 3485
Williamsport, PA 17701

National Baseball Congress
Box 1420
Wichita, KS 62201

U.S.A. Baseball
2160 Greenwood Avenue
Trenton, N.J. 08609

INDEX